Easy Fried Chicken Cookbook

Cookbook

50 Delicious Fried Chicken Recipes

By
BookSumo Press

Published by
http://www.booksumo.com

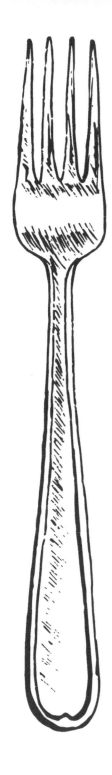

Table of Contents

Crispy Chicken
with Southern Gravy

🥣 Prep Time: 25 mins
🕐 Total Time: 55 mins

Servings per Recipe: 8
Calories	507 kcal
Fat	29 g
Carbohydrates	18.6g
Protein	40.5 g
Cholesterol	142 mg
Sodium	588 mg

Directions

1. In a shallow dish, add the egg and 1/2 C. of milk and beat well.
2. In a resealable plastic bag, combine the flour, poultry seasoning, garlic salt and paprika.
3. Add the chicken pieces and seal the bag.
4. Toss to coat well.
5. Remove the chicken from the bag and transfer the flour mixture into another shallow dish.
6. In a large skillet, heat the oil to 365 degrees F.
7. Dip the chicken into the egg mixture and coat everything in the flour mixture evenly.
8. Reserve the remaining flour mixture.
9. Fry the chicken pieces in the hot oil till browned from all sides.
10. Now reduce the heat to medium-low and cook the chicken pieces for about 30 minutes.
11. Transfer the chicken pieces onto paper towel lined plates to drain.
12. Remove the oil from the skillet, leaving about 2 tbsp in the skillet.
13. Place the skillet on low heat and slowly, add the reserved flour mixture, stirring continuously.
14. Cook everything for about 2 minutes then add the broth, stirring continuously.
15. Increase the heat to high and add the milk, stirring continuously and bring to a boil.
16. Reduce the heat to low and simmer for about 5 minutes.
17. Immediately, pour sauce over the chicken and serve.

Ingredients

1/2 C. milk
1 egg, beaten
1 C. all-purpose flour
2 tsp garlic salt
1 tsp paprika
1 tsp ground black pepper
1/4 tsp poultry seasoning
1 (4 lb.) whole chicken, cut into pieces
3 C. vegetable oil
1 C. chicken broth
1 C. milk

CRISPY GARLICKY
Fried Chicken

Prep Time: 20 mins
Total Time: 35 mins

Servings per Recipe: 4	
Calories	391 kcal
Fat	11.4 g
Carbohydrates	37.3g
Protein	32.8 g
Cholesterol	116 mg
Sodium	935 mg

Ingredients

2 tsp garlic powder
1 tsp ground black pepper
1 tsp salt
1 tsp paprika
1/2 C. seasoned bread crumbs
1 C. all-purpose flour
1/2 C. milk

1 egg
4 skinless, boneless chicken breast halves
1 C. oil for frying, or as needed

Directions

1. In a shallow dish, add the egg and milk and beat well.
2. In another shallow dish mix together the flour, breadcrumbs, garlic powder, paprika, salt and black pepper.
3. Get your oil, in a skillet to 350 degrees F.
4. Dip the chicken breast halves in the egg mixture and then roll in the flour mixture evenly.
5. Fry the chicken breast halves for about 10 minutes, flipping once half way.
6. Serve hot.

Cheesy Parsley Parmesan
Oven Fried Chicken

🥣 Prep Time: 15 mins

🕐 Total Time: 1 hr 30 mins

Servings per Recipe: 6

Calories	607 kcal
Fat	40.4 g
Carbohydrates	13.4g
Protein	45.1 g
Cholesterol	174 mg
Sodium	821 mg

Ingredients

1 clove crushed garlic
1/4 lb. butter, melted
1 C. dried bread crumbs
1/3 C. grated Parmesan cheese
2 tbsp chopped fresh parsley
1 tsp salt
1/8 tsp ground black pepper

1 (4 lb.) chicken, cut into pieces

Directions

1. Set your oven to 350 degrees F before doing anything else and grease a 13x9-inch baking dish.
2. In a shallow dish, mix together the melted butter and garlic.
3. In another shallow dish, mix together the cheese, breadcrumbs, parsley, salt and black pepper.
4. Coat the chicken pieces in the butter mixture and in the cheese mixture evenly.
5. Arrange the chicken pieces into the prepared baking dish in a single layer.
6. Drizzle with the remaining butter mixture evenly and cook everything in the oven for about 1-1 1/4 hours.

BUTTERMILK
Paprika Fried Chicken

Prep Time: 30 mins
Total Time: 50 mins

Servings per Recipe: 8

Calories	489 kcal
Fat	21.8 g
Carbohydrates	29.5g
Protein	40.7 g
Cholesterol	116 mg
Sodium	140 mg

Ingredients

1 (4 lb.) chicken, cut into pieces
1 C. buttermilk
2 C. all-purpose flour for coating
1 tsp paprika
salt and pepper to taste
2 quarts vegetable oil for frying

Directions

1. In a shallow dish, place the buttermilk.
2. In another shallow dish, place the flour, salt, black pepper and paprika.
3. Dip the chicken pieces in the buttermilk completely and coat them in the flour mixture.
4. Arrange the chicken pieces on a baking dish and cover with wax paper and keep aside till flour becomes pasty.
5. In a large cast iron skillet, heat the vegetable oil and fry the chicken pieces till browned.
6. Reduce the heat and cook, covered for about 30 minutes.
7. Uncover and increase the heat and cook till crispy.
8. Transfer the chicken pieces onto paper towel lined plates to drain.

6-Ingredient
Fried Chicken

Prep Time: 15 mins
Total Time: 35 mins

Servings per Recipe: 6
Calories	491 kcal
Fat	32 g
Carbohydrates	16.1g
Protein	32.8 g
Cholesterol	97 mg
Sodium	94 mg

Ingredients

1 (3 lb.) whole chicken, cut into pieces
1 C. all-purpose flour
salt to taste
ground black pepper to taste
1 tsp paprika
1 quart vegetable oil for frying

Directions

1. In a shallow dish, place the flour.
2. Sprinkle the chicken pieces with salt, paprika and black pepper and roll them in the flour evenly.
3. In a large skillet, heat the oil to 365 degrees F.
4. Add the chicken pieces and cook, covered for about 15-20 minutes, flipping once half way.
5. Transfer the chicken pieces onto paper towel lined plates to drain.

INDIAN
Fried Chicken

 Prep Time: 15 mins

Total Time: 1 hr 15 mins

Servings per Recipe: 4

Calories	1238 kcal
Fat	96.3 g
Carbohydrates	13.8g
Protein	85.2 g
Cholesterol	1340 mg
Sodium	1430 mg

Ingredients

1 (4 lb.) whole chicken, cut into pieces
6 cloves garlic, chopped
4 tbsp oyster sauce
2 tbsp curry powder
1/2 C. vegetable oil

Directions

1. In a glass dish, mix together the oyster sauce, garlic and curry powder.
2. Add the chicken pieces and coat it with the mixture generously.
3. Cover and refrigerate for at least 1/2 hour.
4. In a large skillet, heat the oil on medium-high heat and fry the chicken pieces for about 20-25 minutes

Chicken Steaks
with Gravy

🥣 Prep Time: 20 mins
🕐 Total Time: 40 mins

Servings per Recipe: 6
Calories	791 kcal
Fat	34.3 g
Carbohydrates	71.1g
Protein	47 g
Cholesterol	124 mg
Sodium	1393 mg

Ingredients

4 (1/2 lb.) chicken cube steaks
2 C. all-purpose flour
2 tsp baking powder
1 tsp baking soda
1 tsp black pepper
3/4 tsp salt
1 1/2 C. buttermilk

1 egg
1 tbsp hot pepper sauce
2 cloves garlic, minced
3 C. vegetable shortening for deep frying
1/4 C. all-purpose flour
4 C. milk
kosher salt and ground black pepper to taste

Directions

1. With a meat pounder, pound the steaks to 1/4-inch thickness.
2. In a shallow dish, mix together the flour, baking soda, baking powder, salt and black pepper.
3. In another shallow dish, add the egg, buttermilk, hot sauce and garlic and beat well.
4. Coat the steaks with the flour mixture then dip in the egg mixture and again coat with the flour mixture.
5. In a large skillet, heat the oil to 325 degrees F.
6. Add the steaks and fry for about 3-5 minutes on both sides.
7. Transfer the steaks onto paper towel lined plates to drain.
8. Drain the fat from the skillet, reserving about 1/4 C. of the mixture in the skillet.
9. Slowly, add the remaining flour, stirring continuously in the skillet on medium-low heat.
10. Slowly, add the milk, stirring continuously and increase the heat to medium.
11. Bring to a gentle simmer and cook for about 6-7 minutes.
12. Stir in the salt and black pepper and remove from the heat.
13. Pour the gravy over the chicken and serve.

CRISPY
Pheasant

Prep Time: 10 mins
Total Time: 20 mins

Servings per Recipe: 4

Calories	275 kcal
Fat	11.6 g
Carbohydrates	15.3g
Protein	25.8 g
Cholesterol	58 mg
Sodium	243 mg

Ingredients

1 C. milk
1 1/2 tbsp distilled white vinegar
2 pheasant breast halves, thinly sliced
1 C. finely crushed saltine cracker crumbs
1 C. canola oil for frying

Directions

1. In a shallow dish, combine the vinegar and milk.
2. In another shallow dish, place the cracker crumbs.
3. Dip the pheasant slices in the vinegar mixture and then coat everything with the crumbs evenly.
4. In a large skillet, heat the oil on medium-high heat and cook the pheasant slices for about 5 minutes per side.
5. Transfer the pheasant slices onto paper towel lined plates to drain.

Crispy
Fried Chicken Croquettes

Prep Time: 25 mins

Total Time: 2 hr 55 mins

Servings per Recipe: 6	
Calories	377 kcal
Fat	17.5 g
Carbohydrates	26.6g
Protein	27 g
Cholesterol	137 mg
Sodium	765 mg

Ingredients

1/4 C. butter
1/4 C. flour
1/2 C. milk
1/2 C. chicken broth
3 C. finely chopped cooked chicken
1 1/2 C. seasoned bread crumbs, divided
2 eggs, beaten

1/4 C. minced onion
1 tbsp dried parsley
1/4 tsp garlic powder
1/8 tsp celery seed
1/8 tsp cayenne pepper
salt and ground black pepper to taste
1/4 C. oil, or as needed

Directions

1. In a pan, melt the butter on medium heat.
2. Slowly, add the flour, stirring continuously and cook for about 1 minute.
3. Slowly, add the broth and the milk, beating continuously.
4. Cook, stirring continuously for about 5-10 minute till a thick sauce forms.
5. Remove everything from the heat and keep aside for about 10 minutes to cool.
6. In a large bowl, add the cooled sauce, chicken, eggs, 1 C. of the breadcrumbs, onion, parsley, celery seeds, garlic powder, salt and black pepper and mix till well combined.
7. Cover and refrigerate to marinate for about 2 hours.
8. Make 6 equal sized patties from the mixture.
9. In a shallow, dish place the remaining breadcrumbs.
10. Roll the each patty in the breadcrumbs.
11. In a large skillet, heat the oil on medium-high heat and cook the patties for about 5 minutes per side.
12. Transfer the chicken onto paper towel lined plates to drain.

ORIENTAL
Fried Chicken Thighs

Prep Time: 10 mins
Total Time: 8 h 50 mins

Servings per Recipe: 10	
Calories	877 kcal
Fat	68.5 g
Carbohydrates	120.4g
Protein	44 g
Cholesterol	222 mg
Sodium	1137 mg

Ingredients

4 eggs
1/4 C. cornstarch
1/4 C. white sugar
5 cloves garlic, minced
1/2 C. sweet rice flour
4 tsp salt
4 green onions, chopped

1/4 C. oyster sauce
5 lb. boneless chicken thighs, cut in half
2 C. vegetable oil, for deep frying

Directions

1. In a large bowl, mix together all the ingredients except the chicken and oil.
2. Add the chicken pieces and coat them with the mixture generously.
3. Cover and refrigerate everything to marinate overnight.
4. Remove the chicken pieces from the refrigerator and keep everything aside in at room temperature for about 10 minutes before cooking.
5. In a large skillet, heat the oil to 375 degrees F and fry the chicken pieces till golden brown completely.
6. Transfer the chicken pieces onto paper towel lined plates to drain.

Fried Chicken
Stir Fry Dinner

🥘 Prep Time: 30 mins

🕐 Total Time: 1 hr 20 mins

Servings per Recipe: 6	
Calories	700 kcal
Fat	12.1 g
Carbohydrates	76.7g
Protein	67.7 g
Cholesterol	1161 mg
Sodium	1790 mg

Ingredients

2 C. white rice
4 C. water
2/3 C. soy sauce
1/4 C. brown sugar
1 tbsp cornstarch
1 tbsp minced fresh ginger
1 tbsp minced garlic
1/4 tsp red pepper flakes
3 skinless, boneless chicken breast halves, thinly sliced

1 tbsp sesame oil
1 green bell pepper, cut into matchsticks
1 (8 oz.) can sliced water chestnuts, drained
1 head broccoli, broken into florets
1 C. sliced carrots
1 onion, cut into large chunks
1 tbsp sesame oil

Directions

1. In a pan, add the water and rice and bring to a boil on high heat.
2. Reduce the heat to medium-low and simmer, covered for about 20-25 minutes.
3. In a small bowl, add the brown sugar, corn starch and soy sauce and mix till a smooth mixture forms.
4. Add the garlic, ginger and red pepper flakes and mix well.
5. Add the chicken slices and coat everything with the mixture generously.
6. Cover and refrigerate to marinate for about 15-20 minutes.
7. In a large skillet, heat 1 tbsp of the oil on medium-high heat and stir fry the vegetables for about 5 minutes.
8. Transfer the vegetables onto a large plate and cover with some foil to keep them warm.
9. In the same skillet, heat the remaining oil on medium-high heat.
10. Remove the chicken slices from the refrigerator and place the chicken into the skillet, reserving the marinade.
11. Stir fry the chicken for about 2 minutes per side.
12. Add the reserved marinade and the vegetables mixture and bring to a boil.
13. Cook, stirring occasionally for about 5-7 minutes.
14. Serve the chicken mixture over the rice.

FRIED CHICKEN
Livers

Prep Time: 10 mins

Total Time: 20 mins

Servings per Recipe: 4

Calories	470 kcal
Fat	28.9 g
Carbohydrates	27.5g
Protein	24 g
Cholesterol	459 mg
Sodium	186 mg

Ingredients

1 lb. chicken livers
1 egg
1/2 C. milk
1 C. all-purpose flour
1 tbsp garlic powder
salt and pepper to taste
1 quart vegetable oil for frying

Directions

1. In a colander, rinse the chicken livers and keep them aside to drain completely.
2. In a shallow dish, add the milk and egg and beat well.
3. In another shallow dish, place the flour, salt, black pepper and garlic powder.
4. Dip the chicken livers in the milk mixture and then coat them with the flour mixture evenly.
5. In a large skillet, heat the oil to 375 degrees F and fry the chicken livers for about 5-6 minutes.
6. Transfer the chicken livers onto paper towel lined plates to drain.

Thai
Chicken Fried Rice

Prep Time: 30 mins
Total Time: 40 mins

Servings per Recipe: 6
Calories	794 kcal
Fat	22.1 g
Carbohydrates	116.4g
Protein	29.1 g
Cholesterol	46 mg
Sodium	469 mg

Ingredients

3 tbsp oyster sauce
2 tbsp fish sauce
1 tsp white sugar
1/2 C. peanut oil for frying
4 C. cooked jasmine rice, chilled
6 large cloves garlic clove, crushed
2 serrano peppers, crushed

1 lb. boneless, skinless chicken breast, cut into thin strips
1 red pepper, seeded and thinly sliced
1 onion, thinly sliced
2 C. sweet Thai basil
1 cucumber, sliced
1/2 C. cilantro sprigs

Directions

1. In a bowl, add the fish sauce, oyster sauce and sugar and beat till well combined.
2. In a large skillet, heat the oil on medium-high heat and sauté the serrano pepper and garlic for a while.
3. Stir in the chicken strips, sugar mixture, onion and bell pepper and stir fry till the chicken becomes golden brown.
4. Increase the heat to high and add in the rice and stir fry till the rice is blended with the chicken mixture.
5. Stir in the basil and immediately remove everything from the heat.
6. Serve with a garnishing of cucumber and cilantro.

KANAS STYLE
Fried Chicken Cutlets

Prep Time: 10 mins
Total Time: 1 h 45 mins

Servings per Recipe: 4

Calories	481 kcal
Fat	21.5 g
Carbohydrates	49.4g
Protein	22.8 g
Cholesterol	65 mg
Sodium	6378 mg

Ingredients

3 C. cold water
1/4 C. kosher salt
1/4 C. honey
4 boneless skinless chicken breast halves
1/4 C. buttermilk
1 C. all-purpose flour
1 tsp black pepper

1/2 tsp garlic salt
1/2 tsp onion salt
cayenne pepper to taste
vegetable oil for frying

Directions

1. In a large bowl, add the water, honey and salt and mix till the honey is dissolved.
2. Add the chicken breast halves and coat with the honey mixture generously and place a heavy plate over the chicken to submerge it completely.
3. Cover and refrigerate everything to marinate for about 1 hour.
4. Remove the chicken breast halves from the marinade and pat it dry with a paper towel and transfer the meat to a bowl.
5. Add the buttermilk and keep it aside for about 15 minutes.
6. In a shallow dish, place the flour, onion salt, garlic salt, cayenne pepper, salt and black pepper.
7. Coat the chicken breast halves with the flour mixture evenly and arrange everything on a wire rack for about 15 minutes.
8. In a large skillet, heat the oil to 350 degrees F and fry the chicken breast halves for about 15-20 minutes.
9. Transfer the chicken onto paper towel lined plates to drain.

Fried Chicken
In A Japanese Style

Prep Time: 20 mins
Total Time: 1 hr 10 mins

Servings per Recipe: 8	
Calories	256 kcal
Fat	16.7 g
Carbohydrates	4.8g
Protein	20.9 g
Cholesterol	98 mg
Sodium	327 mg

Ingredients

2 eggs, lightly beaten
1/2 tsp salt
1/2 tsp black pepper
1/2 tsp white sugar
1 tbsp minced garlic
1 tbsp grated fresh ginger root
1 tbsp sesame oil

1 tbsp soy sauce
1/8 tsp chicken bouillon granules
1 1/2 lb. skinless, boneless chicken breast halves
- cut into 1 inch cubes
3 tbsp potato starch
1 tbsp rice flour
oil for frying

Directions

1. In a large bowl, add the eggs, gingerroot, garlic, soy sauce, sesame oil, bouillon granules, sugar, salt and black pepper and mix well.
2. Add the chicken cubes and coat them with the mixture generously and refrigerate, covered for about 30 minutes.
3. In a large skillet, heat the oil to 365 degrees F and fry the chicken cubes till golden brown.
4. Transfer the chicken onto paper towel lined plates to drain.

FRIED CHICKEN
Spinach Dinner

Prep Time: 15 mins
Total Time: 1 h

Servings per Recipe: 4

Calories	413 kcal
Fat	17.5 g
Carbohydrates	32.7g
Protein	31.6 g
Cholesterol	70 mg
Sodium	249 mg

Ingredients

1 C. brown rice
2 C. water
1 tbsp olive oil
4 skinless, boneless chicken breast halves, 1/2-inch thick
coarse salt to taste
2 tbsp olive oil

2 cloves garlic, chopped
1 pinch red pepper flakes
1 bunch fresh spinach leaves, trimmed and rinsed
2 tbsp pine nuts
2 tbsp crumbled goat cheese
1/2 lemon, juiced

Directions

1. In a pan, add the water and brown rice and bring to boil.
2. Reduce the heat to medium-low and simmer, covered for about 45-50 minutes.
3. Meanwhile in a large skillet, heat 1 tbsp of the oil on medium heat.
4. Season the chicken with the salt and stir fry everything in the hot oil for about 5-8 minutes on both sides.
5. Transfer the chicken into a plate.
6. In the same skillet, heat the remaining oil and sauté the garlic and red pepper flakes for about 1 minute.
7. Stir in the spinach and cook it for about 2 minutes.
8. Divide the rice between the serving plates and top it with the chicken breasts and spinach evenly.
9. Sprinkle everything with the pine nuts and goat cheese and serve with a drizzling of lemon juice.

Fried Chicken
with Honey Nut Sauce

Prep Time: 15 mins
Total Time: 55 mins

Servings per Recipe: 8
Calories	846 kcal
Fat	59.7 g
Carbohydrates	45.8g
Protein	33.6 g
Cholesterol	194 mg
Sodium	774 mg

Ingredients

1 quart peanut oil for frying
1 whole chicken, cut into 8 pieces
1 tsp seasoned salt
2 eggs, beaten
2 C. self-rising flour
1 pinch salt and ground black pepper
1 C. butter

1/2 C. honey
1 C. chopped pecans

Directions

1. Sprinkle the chicken pieces with the seasoned salt evenly.
2. In a shallow dish, mix together the flour, salt and black pepper.
3. Add the chicken and coat it with the mixture generously.
4. In a large skillet, heat the oil to 375 degrees F and fry the chicken pieces for about 10 minutes on both sides.
5. Transfer the chicken onto paper towel lined plates to drain.
6. In a pan, melt the butter on medium heat and add the honey beating continuously.
7. Cook, beating continuously, for about 5 minutes.
8. Reduce the heat to low and simmer for about 10 minutes.
9. Stir in the pecans and cook for about 2-3 minutes.
10. Pour the honey mixture over the chicken and serve.

SPICY
Fried Chicken Wings 101

🥣 Prep Time: 10 mins

🕐 Total Time: 50 mins

Servings per Recipe: 6

Calories	531 kcal
Fat	41.3 g
Carbohydrates	25.1g
Protein	15.8 g
Cholesterol	37 mg
Sodium	1768 mg

Ingredients

12 small chicken wings
1/4 tsp seasoned salt, or to taste
1 C. all-purpose flour
1 tsp coarse salt
1/2 tsp ground black pepper
1/4 tsp cayenne pepper
1/4 tsp paprika

1 (12 fluid oz.) bottle Buffalo wing sauce
2 quarts vegetable oil for frying

Directions

1. Sprinkle the chicken wings with the seasoned salt evenly.
2. In a shallow dish, mix together the flour, paprika, cayenne pepper, salt and black pepper.
3. Cover and refrigerate to marinate for about 15-30 minutes.
4. In a large skillet, heat the oil to 375 degrees F and fry the chicken wings for about 10 minutes on both sides.
5. Transfer the chicken onto paper towel lined plates to drain.

I ♥ Oven
Fried Chicken

🥄 Prep Time: 30 mins

🕐 Total Time: 1 hr 15 mins

Servings per Recipe: 5

Calories	690 kcal
Fat	53.2 g
Carbohydrates	17.9g
Protein	34.1 g
Cholesterol	114 mg
Sodium	967 mg

Ingredients

1 (2 to 3 lb.) whole chicken, cut into pieces
1 C. dried bread crumbs
1 tsp garlic powder
1 tsp salt
1 tsp ground black pepper
1 tsp dried thyme
1/2 tsp paprika

1 C. mayonnaise

Directions

1. Set your oven to 350 degrees F before doing anything else and lightly, grease a 13x9-inch baking dish.
2. In a shallow dish, mix together the flour, paprika, cayenne pepper, salt and black pepper and mix well.
3. Add the chicken pieces and coat the meat with the mixture generously.
4. Arrange the chicken pieces onto the prepared baking sheet in a single layer.
5. Cook everything in the oven for about 45 minutes.

MARIA'S
Buttermilk Chicken

🥄 Prep Time: 25 mins
🕐 Total Time: 1 d 1 hr

Servings per Recipe: 7
Calories	990 kcal
Fat	82.7 g
Carbohydrates	133.2g
Protein	29.4 g
Cholesterol	98 mg
Sodium	567 mg

Ingredients

1 (3 lb.) whole chicken, cut into pieces
2 C. buttermilk
1 C. dry potato flakes
1 C. all-purpose flour
1 tsp poultry seasoning
1/2 tsp salt
1 tsp freshly ground black pepper

2 C. vegetable oil for frying

Directions

1. In a shallow dish, mix together the chicken pieces and buttermilk.
2. Cover and refrigerate to marinate overnight.
3. In another shallow dish, mix together all the remaining ingredients.
4. Remove the chicken pieces from the buttermilk and coat them with the flour mixture evenly and keep aside for about 15 minutes.
5. In a large skillet, heat the oil to 350 degrees F and fry the chicken pieces till golden brown completely.
6. Transfer the chicken onto paper towel lined plates to drain.

Chicken Tenders 101
with Spicy Dipping Sauce

Prep Time: 30 mins
Total Time: 1 hr

Servings per Recipe: 8

Calories	821 kcal
Fat	55.2 g
Carbohydrates	35.2g
Protein	45.2 g
Cholesterol	164 mg
Sodium	783 mg

Ingredients

1 C. all-purpose flour
2 C. Italian-style seasoned bread crumbs
1/2 tsp ground black pepper
1/2 tsp cayenne pepper
2 eggs, beaten
2 tbsp water
24 chicken tenderloins

2 quarts oil for frying
1 C. mayonnaise
3 tbsp prepared horseradish
1/2 C. sour cream
1 dash Worcestershire sauce
3 tbsp prepared mustard

Directions

1. In a shallow dish, place the flour.
2. In a second shallow dish, beat together the water and eggs.
3. In a third shallow dish, mix together the breadcrumbs, cayenne pepper and black pepper.
4. First coat the chicken tenderloins in the flour, followed by the egg mixture and the breadcrumb mixture.
5. In a large skillet, heat the oil to 375 degrees F and fry the chicken tenderloins for about 6-8 minutes.
6. Meanwhile for the dipping sauce, in a bowl, mix together the remaining ingredients.
7. Transfer the chicken onto paper towel lined plates to drain.
8. Serve the chicken with the dipping sauce.

PERFECT GLUTEN-FREE
Chicken Cutlets

🥄 Prep Time: 10 mins

🕐 Total Time: 30 mins

Servings per Recipe: 6

Calories	261 kcal
Fat	12.2 g
Carbohydrates	1.8g
Protein	34.2 g
Cholesterol	93 mg
Sodium	446 mg

Ingredients

2 C. oil
1 C. gluten-free all-purpose flour
2 tsp powdered buttermilk
1 tsp paprika
1 tsp celery salt
1/2 tsp ground white pepper
1/2 tsp xanthan gum

1/2 tsp baking soda
1/4 tsp cayenne pepper
2 lb. skinless, boneless chicken breast halves

Directions

1. In a large shallow dish, mix together all the ingredients except the chicken breast halves and the oil.
2. Add the chicken breast halves and coat them with the mixture generously.
3. In a large skillet, heat the oil to 375 degrees F and fry the chicken tenderloins for about 5 minutes per side.
4. Transfer the chicken onto paper towel lined plates to drain.

Memphis
Fried Chicken Breasts

Prep Time: 30 mins
Total Time: 8 hr 35 mins

Servings per Recipe: 8
Calories	635 kcal
Fat	22.7 g
Carbohydrates	69.4g
Protein	37.1 g
Cholesterol	258 mg
Sodium	3112 mg

Ingredients

8 skinless, boneless chicken breast halves, pounded to 3/4-inch thickness
1 quart buttermilk
3 shallots, finely chopped
2 tbsp chopped garlic
2 tbsp salt
2 tbsp white sugar

1 1/4 tsp ground cumin
1 1/2 tsp ground black pepper
2 C. vegetable oil for frying
4 C. all-purpose flour
2 tbsp baking powder
2 tsp salt
8 large eggs, beaten

Directions

1. In a resealable bag, mix together the buttermilk, garlic, shallots, sugar, cumin, salt and black pepper.
2. Add the chicken breast halves and tightly, seal the bag and shake to coat well.
3. Refrigerate to marinate overnight.
4. In a shallow dish, mix together the flour, baking powder and salt.
5. In another shallow dish, add the eggs.
6. Remove the chicken breast halves from the refrigerator and shake off the excess marinade.
7. First, coat the chicken breast halves in the flour mixture, then dip everything into the eggs and again coat them with the flour mixture.
8. In a large skillet, heat the oil on medium heat and fry the chicken breasts halves for about 2-3 minutes per side.
9. Transfer the chicken onto paper towel lined plates to drain.

ITALIAN TOMATO
Fried Chicken

🥣 Prep Time: 5 mins
🕐 Total Time: 40 mins

Servings per Recipe: 7	
Calories	740 kcal
Fat	45.4 g
Carbohydrates	25.1g
Protein	53.8 g
Cholesterol	1250 mg
Sodium	767 mg

Ingredients

2 eggs, beaten
2/3 C. milk
1 1/2 C. all-purpose flour
1 (.7 oz.) package dry Italian-style salad dressing mix
1 packet dry tomato soup mix
1 (4 lb.) whole chicken, cut into pieces
2 tbsp vegetable oil

Directions

1. In a shallow dish, beat together the eggs and milk.
2. In another dish, mix together the remaining ingredients except the chicken and the oil.
3. Dip the chicken pieces in the egg mixture and roll them in the flour mixture evenly.
4. In a large skillet, heat the oil on medium-high heat and fry the chicken pieces for about 25-35 minutes, flipping occasionally.
5. Transfer the chicken onto paper towel lined plates to drain.

Curry
Fried Chicken

🥄 Prep Time: 15 mins

🕐 Total Time: 20 mins

Servings per Recipe: 5

Calories	177 kcal
Fat	7.1 g
Carbohydrates	5.2g
Protein	21.9 g
Cholesterol	53 mg
Sodium	102 mg

Ingredients

2 tbsp vegetable oil
1 lb. skinless, boneless chicken breast halves
1 onion, sliced
1 tsp ginger garlic paste
2 green chili peppers, chopped
3 tsp ground coriander seed
1 tsp garam masala

1/2 tsp ground turmeric
1 tsp chili powder
1 pinch ground allspice
1 tbsp fresh chopped cilantro, for garnish
salt to taste

Directions

1. In a pan, heat the oil and stir fry the green chili pepper, onion, ginger-garlic paste and garam masala powder till the onion becomes golden brown.
2. Stir in the chicken pieces, allspice, chili powder, turmeric and black pepper and stir fry it for about 5-6 minutes.
3. Stir in the coriander powder and salt and fry it till the desired doneness.
4. Serve with a garnishing of cilantro.

EASY MEXICAN
Fried Chicken Chimichangas

Prep Time: 20 mins
Total Time: 45 mins

Servings per Recipe: 1	
Calories	353.9
Fat	16.8g
Cholesterol	46.0mg7
Sodium	17.8mg
Carbohydrates	31.4g
Protein	18.7g

Ingredients

2/3 C. your favorite salsa
1 tsp ground cumin
1/2 tsp dried oregano leaves, crushed
1 1/2 C. cooked chicken, chopped
1 C. shredded cheddar cheese
2 green onions, chopped with some tops
6 (8 inch) flour tortillas

2 tbsp margarine, melted
shredded cheddar cheese, for serving
chopped green onion, for serving
picante sauce, for serving

Directions

1. Set your oven to 400 degrees F before doing anything else.
2. In a bowl, mix together the chicken, salsa, cheese, green onions, oregano and cumin.
3. Divide about 1/4 C. of the chicken mixture in the center of the each tortilla.
4. Roll each tortilla to seal the filling.
5. Arrange the rolls onto a baking sheet in a single layer, seam-side down and coat with the melted margarine evenly.
6. Cook everything in the oven for about 25 minutes.
7. Serve with a garnishing of cheese and green onion alongside the remaining chicken mixture.

Glamorous
Fried Chicken

Prep Time: 15 mins
Total Time: 1 hr 15 mins

Servings per Recipe: 4
Calories	1006.5
Fat	71.4g
Cholesterol	1307.9mg
Sodium	1899.5mg
Carbohydrates	14.6g
Protein	72.5g

Ingredients

2/3 C. breadcrumbs
2/3 C. grated parmesan cheese
1/4 C. minced fresh parsley
1/4 tsp salt
1/8 tsp fresh ground pepper
5 tbsp butter
3 garlic cloves, minced

3 lb. chicken, cut up

Directions

1. Set your oven to 350 degrees F before doing anything else and line a baking sheet with foil.
2. In a pan, add the butter and garlic on very low heat and cook till the butter is melted then remove everything from the heat.
3. In a shallow dish, mix together the cheese, breadcrumbs, parsley, salt and black pepper.
4. Coat the chicken pieces with the butter and then roll everything into the cheese mixture evenly.
5. Arrange the chicken pieces onto the prepared baking sheet in a single layer, skin-side up.
6. In a bowl, mix together the remaining butter mixture and cheese mixture and place the mix over the chicken pieces evenly.
7. Cook everything in the oven for about 1 hour.

FRIED CHICKEN
with Pesto

🥄 Prep Time: 10 mins
🕐 Total Time: 30 mins

Servings per Recipe: 4
Calories   200.4
Fat   4.4g
Cholesterol   108.9mg
Sodium   210.1mg
Carbohydrates   1.5g
Protein   36.2g

Ingredients

1 1/2 l. boneless skinless chicken breasts
3 tbsp purchased pesto sauce
1/4 C. corn flake crumbs

Directions

1. Set your oven to 375 degrees F before doing anything else.
2. In a shallow dish, place the pesto.
3. In another shallow dish, place the crumbs.
4. Coat the chicken fillets with the pesto evenly and roll it in the crumbs.
5. Place the chicken fillets on a nonstick baking sheet and cook everything in the oven for about 15-20 minutes.

South Carolina
Secret Fried Chicken

🥣 Prep Time: 10 mins
🕐 Total Time: 1 hr

Servings per Recipe: 3
Calories	1134.6
Fat	76.6g
Cholesterol	1350.9mg
Sodium	11609.0mg
Carbohydrates	18.7g
Protein	86.8g

Ingredients

3 lb. chicken, cut up
2/3 C. biscuit mix
1 tbsp butter
1 1/4 tsp salt
1 1/2 tsp paprika
1/4 tsp pepper

Directions

1. Set your oven to 425 degrees F before doing anything else.
2. In a 13x9-inch baking dish, add the butter and place everything in the oven to melt.
3. In a shallow dish mix together the remaining ingredients except the chicken pieces.
4. Coat the chicken pieces with the mixture evenly and place everything in the baking dish with the melted butter, skin-side down.
5. Cook everything in the oven for about 50 minutes, flipping once after 45 minutes.

FRIED CHICKEN
in College

Prep Time: 15 mins
Total Time: 1 hr

Servings per Recipe: 4
Calories	224.9
Fat	8.8g
Cholesterol	75.5mg
Sodium	570.0mg
Carbohydrates	9.7g
Protein	25.8g

Ingredients

4 boneless skinless chicken breasts
1 1/2 C. corn flakes, made into about 3/4 C. crumbs
2 tbsp melted margarine
2 tbsp lemon juice
1/2 tsp salt
1/8 tsp pepper
nonstick cooking spray

Directions

1. Set your oven to 375 degrees F before doing anything else and grease a baking sheet.
2. In a shallow dish, mix together the lemon juice, margarine, salt and black pepper.
3. In another shallow dish, add the cornflakes crumbs.
4. Dip the chicken breasts in the margarine mixture and coat them with the crumbs evenly.
5. Arrange the chicken breasts onto the prepared baking sheet in a single layer.
6. Cook everything in the oven for about 45 minutes.

Chipotle
Baked Fried Chicken

🥣 Prep Time: 1 hr
🕐 Total Time: 1 hr 50 mins

Servings per Recipe: 6
Calories	527.1
Fat	21.9g
Cholesterol	151.9mg
Sodium	448.4mg
Carbohydrates	29.1g
Protein	49.7g

Ingredients

2 whole canned chipotle chilies in adobo
3/4 C. mayonnaise
6 chicken drumsticks
6 chicken breasts
2 1/4 C. breadcrumbs
1/4 tsp cayenne pepper
salt and pepper

Directions

1. In a food processor, add mayonnaise, chipotle chili, salt and black pepper and pulse till smooth.
2. In a baking dish, place the mayo mixture and coat the chicken drumsticks generously then arrange everything in a single layer.
3. Cover and refrigerate to marinate for about 1 hour.
4. Set your oven to 425 degrees F.
5. In a shallow dish, mix together the remaining ingredients.
6. Remove the chicken drumsticks from the marinade and coat everything with the breadcrumb mixture evenly.
7. Arrange the chicken drumsticks on the roasting rack and cook everything in the oven for about 30 minutes, flipping once half way.
8. Now, set the oven to 375 degrees F and cook the contents for about 15 minutes more.

CHINESE TAKE-OUT
Fried Chicken

🥣 Prep Time: 10 mins

🕐 Total Time: 1 hr 10 mins

Servings per Recipe: 1

Calories	1237.1
Fat	122.6g
Cholesterol	178.6mg
Sodium	855.1mg
Carbohydrates	18.0g
Protein	18.3g

Ingredients

1 egg, beaten
2 C. milk
2 C. all-purpose flour
4 tsp salt
2 tsp black pepper
1 tsp MSG (monosodium glutamate) (optional)
6 C. Crisco cooking oil

2 frying chickens, with skin, each cut into 6 pieces

Directions

1. In a shallow dish, add the milk and eggs and beat well.
2. In another shallow dish, mix together the remaining ingredients except the chicken pieces and the oil.
3. Dip the chicken pieces in the egg mixture and then the flour mixture evenly.
4. In a large pressure fryer, heat the oil to 400 degrees F.
5. Stir in the chicken pieces (in batches) and tightly, lock the lid.
6. Set the time for about 10 minutes after the steam just starts to shoot through the pressure release.
7. Release the pressure according to manufacturer's directions.

Almond
Baked Fried Chicken

Prep Time: 20 mins
Total Time: 40 mins

Servings per Recipe: 6
Calories	329.1
Fat	20.8g
Cholesterol	50.0mg
Sodium	649.2mg
Carbohydrates	14.6g
Protein	20.4g

Ingredients

1 C. fresh processed breadcrumbs
1/4 C. grated parmesan cheese
1/4 C. almonds, finely chopped
2 tbsp chopped fresh parsley
1 minced garlic clove
1/4 tsp dried thyme
1 tsp salt

1/4 tsp black pepper
1/4 C. olive oil
6 chicken breast halves, pounded to 1/2 inch thickness

Directions

1. Set your oven to 400 degrees F before doing anything else and grease a baking sheet.
2. In a shallow dish, place the oil.
3. In another shallow dish, mix together the remaining ingredients except the chicken breast halves.
4. Dip the chicken breast halves in the oil and coat them with the cheese mixture evenly.
5. Arrange the chicken breast halves onto the prepared baking sheet in a single layer.
6. Cook everything in the oven for about 20 minutes.

DIJON
Fried Chicken

Prep Time: 1 day

Total Time: 1 day 15 mins

Servings per Recipe: 4

Calories	3698.3
Fat	323.8g
Cholesterol	4329.5mg
Sodium	13791.3mg
Carbohydrates	183.3g
Protein	116.4g

Ingredients

2 C. buttermilk
1/4 C. Dijon mustard
2 tbsp onion powder with green onion and parsley
5 tsp salt
4 tsp dry mustard
4 tsp cayenne pepper
2 1/2 tsp ground black pepper

1 (3 1/4 lb.) fryer chickens, backbone removed and chicken cut into 8 pieces with skin removed (except wings)
3 C. all-purpose flour
1 tbsp baking powder
1 tbsp garlic powder
5 C. peanut oil

Directions

1. In a large resealable bag, mix together the Dijon mustard, buttermilk, 1 tsp of dry mustard, 1 tbsp of onion powder, 1 tsp of cayenne pepper and 1 tsp of both, salt and black pepper.
2. Add the chicken pieces and seal the bag tightly then shake the bag to coat well.
3. Refrigerate for about 1-2 days, flipping occasionally.
4. In a large shallow, dish mix together the remaining ingredients.
5. Remove the chicken pieces from the marinade and coat them with the flour mixture evenly.
6. Keep the pieces in the flour mixture for about 1 hour, turning them in the mixture occasionally.
7. In a large skillet, heat the oil to 350 degrees F and place the chicken pieces, skin-side down.
8. Reduce the heat to maintain the temperature of the oil between 280 degrees F to 300 degrees F and fry the chicken pieces for about 5 minutes.
9. Flip each piece and fry for about 7 minutes.
10. Then flip each piece again and fry for about 3 minutes.
11. With a slotted spoon, place the chicken pieces over a wire rack.
12. Transfer the chicken pieces onto paper towel lined plates to drain.

Texas Ranch
Fried Chicken

Prep Time: 15 mins
Total Time: 55 mins

Servings per Recipe: 3	
Calories	650.2
Fat	36.3g
Cholesterol	175.8mg
Sodium	913.3mg
Carbohydrates	31.8g
Protein	46.7g

Ingredients

6 chicken thighs, cutlets bone and skin off
1 C. buttermilk
1/2 envelope original ranch dressing mix
4 tsp hot sauce
1 C. dry breadcrumbs
1/2 C. grated parmesan cheese
2 tsp paprika

1 tsp garlic salt
1/2 tsp cayenne
1/2 tsp dried thyme
1/2 tsp dried oregano
cooking spray, to cook

Directions

1. With a fork, prick the thigh cutlets completely.
2. In a large bowl, mix together the ranch dressing, buttermilk and the hot sauce.
3. Refrigerate to marinate for about 1 hour.
4. Set your oven to 395 degrees F and grease a baking sheet with cooking spray.
5. In a shallow dish, mix together the remaining ingredients and coat the chicken cutlets with the mixture evenly.
6. Arrange the chicken cutlets onto the prepared baking sheet in a single layer.
7. Cook everything in the oven for about 40 minutes.
8. Now, set the oven to 355 degrees F and cook for about 10 minutes more.

HOW TO THROW TOGETHER
Fried Chicken

🥣 Prep Time: 20 mins

🕐 Total Time: 1 hr 20 mins

Servings per Recipe: 6

Calories	328.8
Fat	20.9 g
Cholesterol	110.9 mg
Sodium	532.9 mg
Carbohydrates	16.5 g
Protein	17.6 g

Ingredients

1 cut up chicken
1 beaten egg
1/2 C. milk
1 tsp salt
1/8 tsp pepper
1 C. cracker crumb
4 tbsp butter

Directions

1. Set your oven to 325 degrees F before doing anything else
2. In a shallow dish, add the egg and milk and beat well.
3. In another shallow dish, mix together the cracker crumb, salt and black pepper.
4. Dip the chicken pieces in the egg mixture and then roll them in the crumb mixture evenly.
5. In a large ovenproof skillet, melt the butter and fry the chicken till golden brown on both sides.
6. Now, transfer the skillet to the oven and cook, covered for about 30 minutes.
7. Uncover and cook everything in the oven for about 30 minutes more.

Fried
Chicken Salad

Prep Time: 10 mins
Total Time: 20 mins

Servings per Recipe: 3	
Calories	221.6
Fat	13.9g
Cholesterol	125.3mg
Sodium	365.9mg
Carbohydrates	4.2g
Protein	19.0g

Ingredients

1 head iceberg lettuce, torn
3 eggs
1 lb. of frozen chicken tenders
1 C. shredded cheese
1/2 C. ranch dressing
3 tsp of favorite barbecue sauce
crouton

tomatoes
1 cucumber

Directions

1. Boil the eggs and keep them aside to cool completely then chop them.
2. Cook the chicken tenders in the oven according to package's directions and then cut into bite size pieces.
3. In a bowl, mix together the chicken, chopped eggs, cheese, lettuce, cucumber and tomato.
4. In another bowl, mix together the barbecue sauce and ranch dressing.
5. Place the dressing mixture over the salad and serve.

CHICKEN TENDERS
III

🥄 Prep Time: 20 mins
🕐 Total Time: 35 mins

Servings per Recipe: 2
Calories   2548.7
Fat   233.0g
Cholesterol   3428.5mg
Sodium   1386.7mg
Carbohydrates   51.5g
Protein   65.4g

Ingredients

1 lb. chicken tenders
1 C. all-purpose flour
3 eggs
1 tbsp season salt
1/2 tbsp red pepper flakes
1/2 tbsp black pepper
1/4 C. milk

2 C. canola oil

Directions

1. In a shallow dish, mix together the flour, red pepper flakes, seasoned salt and black pepper.
2. In another shallow dish, add the egg and milk and beat well.
3. Roll the chicken tenders in the flour mixture, then dip them in the egg mixture and again roll them in the flour mixture evenly.
4. In a large skillet, heat the oil and fry the chicken for about 5-7 minutes on both sides.
5. Transfer the chicken pieces onto paper towel lined plates to drain.

Spicy
Cornmeal Fried Chicken

🥣 Prep Time: 10 mins
🕐 Total Time: 45 mins

Servings per Recipe: 4
Calories	152.4
Fat	3.3g
Cholesterol	75.5mg
Sodium	429.8mg
Carbohydrates	3.7g
Protein	25.5g

Ingredients

2 tbsp cornmeal
1 tsp paprika
1/2 tsp salt
1/2 tsp garlic powder
1/2 tsp pepper
1/4 tsp cumin, ground
4 medium boneless skinless chicken breast halves

nonstick cooking spray

Directions

1. In a large bowl, mix together all the ingredients except the chicken and cooking spray.
2. Add the chicken breast halves and coat them with the mixture generously.
3. Grease a nonstick skillet with the cooking spray and heat them on medium heat.
4. Cook the chicken breast halves for about 8-10 minutes, flipping occasionally.

45-MINUTE
Fried Chicken

Prep Time: 5 mins
Total Time: 45 mins

Servings per Recipe: 4
Calories   698.5
Fat   53.5g
Cholesterol   129.3mg
Sodium   412.1mg
Carbohydrates   18.2g
Protein   34.5g

Ingredients

3/4 C. all-purpose flour
1/2 tsp garlic salt
1/2 tsp salt
1/2 tsp celery salt
1/2 tsp pepper
1/2 tsp paprika
2 1/2-3 lb. chicken pieces

1/2 C. canola oil

Directions

1. In a shallow dish, mix together all the ingredients except the chicken and the canola oil.
2. Add the chicken pieces and coat them with the mixture evenly.
3. In a large skillet, heat the oil to 365 degrees F and fry the chicken pieces till golden brown.
4. Transfer the chicken pieces onto paper towel lined plates to drain.

Boardwalk
Fried Chicken

Prep Time: 30 mins
Total Time: 40 mins

Servings per Recipe: 4
Calories   949.8
Fat   56.8g
Cholesterol   298.8mg
Sodium   993.2mg
Carbohydrates   39.1g
Protein   65.6g

Ingredients

1 medium whole chicken, cut into serving pieces
1 1/2 C. flour, sifted
1 tsp salt
pepper, to taste
1 1/2 tsp baking powder
1 egg
1 C. milk

fat or oil, for frying

Directions

1. Steam the chicken till tender.
2. Keep aside to cool and with a paper towel, pat dry.
3. In a shallow dish, mix together all the remaining ingredients and coat the chicken pieces with the mixture evenly.
4. In a large skillet, heat the oil to 380 degrees F and fry the chicken pieces till golden brown.

MEXICO CITY
Chili Lime Fried Chicken

Prep Time: 12 hr
Total Time: 12 hr 40 mins

Servings per Recipe: 4

Calories	762.8
Fat	48.2g
Cholesterol	200.9mg
Sodium	640.2mg
Carbohydrates	31.0g
Protein	49.1g

Ingredients

1 broiler-fryer chicken, cut-up
1 (8 oz.) cartons sour cream
1/4 C. milk
1 (4 oz.) cans diced green chili peppers
2 tbsp fresh cilantro
2 tbsp lime juice
1 garlic clove

1 tsp ground cumin
3/4 tsp salt
1/4 tsp black pepper
1 C. all-purpose flour
lime wedge

Directions

1. In a large bowl, mix together all the ingredients except chicken, flour and the lime wedges.
2. Add the chicken pieces and coat them with the mixture generously.
3. Cover and refrigerate the meat to marinate overnight, flipping occasionally.
4. In a shallow dish, place the flour and coat the chicken pieces with the flour evenly.
5. In a large skillet, heat the oil to 350 degrees F.
6. Reduce the heat to medium and fry the chicken pieces for about 40 minutes, stirring occasionally.
7. Transfer the chicken pieces onto paper towel lined plates to drain.
8. Serve with a garnishing of lemon wedges.

Rainy Day Oven
Fried Chicken

🥣 Prep Time: 4 hr 30 mins

🕐 Total Time: 5 hr 25 mins

Servings per Recipe: 6

Calories	241.5
Fat	12.4g
Cholesterol	65.1mg
Sodium	432.2mg
Carbohydrates	13.9g
Protein	18.4g

Ingredients

2 1/2 lb. skinless chicken pieces
3/4 C. mayonnaise, can use lowfat but not fat free
1 tbsp lemon juice
1/4-1/2 tsp salt
1 tsp Worcestershire sauce
1/8-1/4 tsp hot sauce
1/2 tsp garlic powder

1/2 tsp celery salt
1/2 tsp dry mustard
1/4 tsp pepper
1/4 tsp sweet paprika
1 1/2 C. crushed corn flakes
2 tbsp chopped parsley

Directions

1. In a large bowl, mix together all the ingredients except the chicken, cornflakes and the parsley.
2. Add the chicken pieces and coat them with the mixture generously.
3. Cover and refrigerate to marinate for about 4-24 hours.
4. Set your oven to 350 degrees F.
5. In a shallow dish, place the cornflakes and parsley and coat the chicken pieces with the mixture evenly.
6. Cook everything in the oven for about 45-55 minutes.

PARALLEL PROCESSING
Fried Chicken

🥣 Prep Time: 10 mins

🕐 Total Time: 1 hr 10 mins

Servings per Recipe: 4
Calories	634.0
Fat	45.7g
Cholesterol	170.7mg
Sodium	305.3mg
Carbohydrates	10.0g
Protein	43.5g

Ingredients

1/4 C. margarine
1 C. instant potato flakes
1/2 tsp garlic salt
1/2 tsp seasoned pepper
1/2 tsp seasoning salt
2 - 3 lb. frying chickens, cut up

Directions

1. Set your oven to 400 degrees F before doing anything else.
2. Place the margarine in a 13x9-inch baking dish and keep it in the oven till melted.
3. In a large bowl, mix together all the ingredients and coat the chicken pieces with the mixture generously.
4. Arrange the chicken pieces in the baking dish of melted margarine, skin-side down.
5. Cook everything in the oven for about 60 minutes, turning once.

Mumbai
Fried Chicken

🥣 Prep Time: 10 mins
🕐 Total Time: 35 mins

Servings per Recipe: 4
Calories   484.3
Fat   23.9g
Cholesterol   148.7mg
Sodium   170.9mg
Carbohydrates   28.5g
Protein   36.2g

Ingredients

4 chicken drumsticks
4 chicken thighs
Marinade
2 tsp curry powder
1 garlic clove, finely minced
1/2 tsp ground black pepper
1/2 tsp paprika

Coating
1 1/4 C. milk
1 C. flour
oil, for frying

Directions

1. In a large baking dish, mix together all the marinade ingredients.
2. Add the chicken pieces and coat them with the mixture generously.
3. Cover and refrigerate to marinate for about 12 hours.
4. Set your oven to 350 degrees F.
5. Remove the baking dish from the refrigerator and place the milk and keep it aside for about 15-20 minutes.
6. In a shallow dish, place the flour.
7. Discard the milk from the marinade and coat the chicken pieces with the flour evenly.
8. In a skillet, heat a little oil and fry the chicken pieces till golden brown.
9. Transfer the chicken pieces into a baking dish and cook everything in the oven for about 35-40 minutes

BATON ROUGE EASY
Fried Chicken

🥄 Prep Time: 10 mins

🕐 Total Time: 30 mins

Servings per Recipe: 4

Calories	472.5
Fat	20.6g
Cholesterol	131.5mg
Sodium	123.3mg
Carbohydrates	24.2g
Protein	44.1g

Ingredients

1 C. all-purpose flour
3 tbsp salt-free cajun spice
1 tsp coarse grind black pepper
1 (2-3 lb.) whole fryer chicken, cut up backbone
removed
Lawry's Seasoned Salt
ground black pepper

vegetable oil

Directions

1. Sprinkle the chicken pieces with the seasoned salt and ground black pepper evenly.
2. In a large shallow dish, mix together the flour, Cajun spice and grinded black pepper.
3. Add the chicken pieces and coat them with the mixture generously.
4. In a baking dish, place the chicken pieces and keep them aside for about 1 hour, sprinkle the pieces with the remaining flour occasionally.
5. In a large skillet, heat the oil and fry the chicken pieces for about 8 minutes on both sides.
6. Transfer the chicken pieces onto paper towel lined plates to drain.
7. Serve with your desired side dish.

Mr Tokyo's
Fried Chicken

Prep Time: 2 hr 30 mins
Total Time: 3 hrs

Servings per Recipe: 4
Calories	1884.0
Fat	188.1g
Cholesterol	2129.3mg
Sodium	1206.7mg
Carbohydrates	13.7g
Protein	34.7g

Ingredients

2 1/2-3 lb. chicken, cut in 8 pieces and chop into 2-inch pieces across the bones
2 tbsp soy sauce
1 tbsp apple cider
1 tsp salt
1/2 tsp sugar
1 scallion, cut into 2 inch pieces and split in half

1/2 inch gingerroot, crushed
3 C. peanut oil
1/2 C. flour

Directions

1. In a large bowl, add the gingerroot, scallion, sugar, apple cider, soy sauce and salt and mix till sugar is dissolved.
2. Add the chicken pieces and coat them with the mixture generously and keep them aside for about 1-2 hours in room temperature.
3. Remove the chicken pieces from the bowl and discard the marinade.
4. With a paper towel, pat dry the chicken pieces.
5. In a deep fryer, heat the oil to 375 degrees F on medium-high heat.
6. In a shallow dish, place the flour.
7. Coat the chicken pieces with the flour evenly.
8. Fry the chicken pieces in hot oil for about 5 minutes, turning occasionally.
9. Transfer the chicken onto paper towel lined plates to drain.

Printed in Great Britain
by Amazon